Becoming Ebony

CRAB ORCHARD AWARD SERIES IN POETRY

Becoming Ebony

PATRICIA JABBEH WESLEY

Crab Orchard Review

& Southern Illinois University Press

Carbondale and Edwardsville

The Crab Orchard Award Series in Poetry is a joint publishing venture of
Southern Illinois University Press and *Crab Orchard Review*. This series has been
made possible by the generous support of the Office of the President of Southern Illinois
University and the Office of the Vice Chancellor for Academic Affairs and Provost at
Southern Illinois University Carbondale.

Crab Orchard Award Series in Poetry Editor: Jon Tribble
Judge for 2002: Tim Seibles

Library of Congress Cataloging-in-Publication Data

Wesley, Patricia Jabbeh.
  Becoming ebony / Patricia Jabbeh Wesley.
    p. cm. — (Crab Orchard award series in poetry)
  1. Liberian Americans—Poetry. I. Title. II. Series.
  PS3573.E915 B43 2003
  811'.54—dc21
  ISBN 0-8093-2517-9 (pbk. : alk. paper)   2002010912

Printed on recycled paper.

The paper used in this publication meets the minimum requirements of
American National Standard for Information Sciences—Permanence of Paper
for Printed Library Materials, ANSI Z39.48-1992. ∞

In Memory of My Mother:

Hne Dahtedor, tall woman from Dolokeh, the hill country.
People in the ruined city called you Mary Williams.
When *Iyeeh* sang praise songs to you, she called you
Wlansu Dahtedor, *Hne-a-ju*, mother of children, *Koo-o-koo*.

Contents

Four

Acknowledgments

Poems in this book or excerpts have appeared or are forthcoming in the following literary journals and anthologies:

The Cortland Review—"In the Beginning" and "This Is What I Tell My Daughter"

Crab Orchard Review—"Elegy to West Point Fishermen," "I Now Wander," and "I Used to Own This Town"

Encore Magazine—"Around the Mountains" and "In This Town"

Karamu—"We've Done It All"

Midday Moon—"They Want to Rise Up," "All the Soft Things of Earth," "For My Husband," and "War Baby"

The Moon Day Reader—"In This Town"

New Orleans Review—"Around the Mountains" and "Get Out of Here, Boys!"

New Sister Voices: Poetry by American Women of African Descent— "Elegy to West Point Fishermen," "Get Out of Here, Boys!" and "I Now Wander"

I wish to thank the Kalamazoo Community Foundation for awarding an ArtFund Grant through the Arts Council of Greater Kalamazoo, which allowed me time to complete this book.

Finally, I'd like to acknowledge that this book could not have been written without the support of my husband, Mlen-Too, and my four lovely children, Besie-Nyesuah, M-T, Gee, and Ade-Juah Wesley.

One

My Birth at the Doorpost

In the birthing chamber, an old lady stands
at the doorpost where *Iyeeh* and other village
women are bending over Mama who is pushing
me out into the world. Someone is giving

commands about how the baby's head must
be pushed out. Mama sits hollering so hard
and crying so loud, I can hardly hear anything
else. There are mumbling voices in the background.

Another old lady, who knows everything about
everything, stands there at Mama's feet. She is
spitting out commands about the cutting of
the navel string so nothing is left inside Mama.

They say a woman like her can't be tied down
forever to her first child by an umbilical cord.
It is an abomination to die in childbirth. It is an
abomination to die giving birth to your first child.

So I come out screaming, head first, the way they
wished me out. If they had asked me, I would
have come out legs first, then hands before head.
So I can run away from home someday.

I Used to Own This Town

This place used to be my town . . . even when
the river rose from its own bed, taking up residence

with us in the rainy season, hiding under our beds
and dining tables; in kitchens, bathrooms, and

the town's pots and pans went sailing past us like
speed boats in the rain. Then we children splashed

about while our Mamas wept for mattresses
and pictures and all those memories floating away.

In the dry season, we ran in between houses, ponytails
and flat chests, panties or just bikinis, bare feet

and nappy hair, turning red from the dust and heat.
Then all the boys, in shorts, would dash with us

into Auntie Vic's big, black tub—until one day, I figured
out how to make her son, Mikey, breathe under

the tub full of water. All I wanted was to see how
a boy can breathe under water, and Mama comes

with rattan, giving me such a whipping . . . Slip Way,
loud Accra bars where Ghana High-Life-Beat

ran away with the night while we slept. Slip Way
was my town—where you could slip away, sit beside

the river and watch giant crabs and *gbuga* fish
swim around you. Up Crown Hill, no one guessed

we were hiding beneath that hill. Monrovia rushed
away without us. Did Monrovia know we owned

the river down there? Where the town humps like
a weary camel, we owned the hill, the sloping,

hanging rocks, clinging on tightly to the hill; we
owned the river, the fish and the kiss-meat shells.

The sun returned home at dusk, and we children
were running all over the place, hollering, and our

Mamas couldn't tell their own voices calling us home—
we were singing and laughing at how we could scare

a Mama out of her breath. And all the fathers coming
home, sweaty, oily faces, rough concrete hands.

At night, *Yana Boys* came home too, from Waterside
marketplaces—the bursting sewage coming back

to town, the smell of fish. We owned all the dust,
the rocky hills, and all that poverty. So much laughing,

the giving and taking with everybody into everybody,
into everybody's business. When the moon came out

at night, we ran to the street, giggling. One long,
crooked line, marching, as the moon followed us.

Get Out of Here, Boys!

When we were children, we lived in Slip Way, Bishop
Brooks or Bassa Community, laid out, the masterpieces

of an unskilled artist. We were Turtur and Muriel and Mikey,
Comfort and Teeta, Sunday and me. Me, thin like a needle,

and my friend, Turtur, looking like she would break in half.
It was not just the houses matted into each other, not just their

zinc roofs touching, not just grass running from one door to
the other, too many pots boiling in one big kitchen. It was not

just us children in the rain, playing *Rain, Rain, Come Down,*
or *Nafoot* or *I Was Passing By, My Auntie Called Me In.*

It was something, you see, just something. The boys running
around, shirtless. Little sticks for guns under skinny arms, in

between houses, chasing an enemy, playing *Cowboy War;*
but we girls, in our corners, bamboo sticks for people,

cardboard boxes for gates, playing *Family*—Then the boys
came running, feet too big for shoes, barefoot, stomping over

our make-believe houses, our bamboo people. Sun so hot it
could set the whole world on fire, and there they were, shouting,

"Kpaw, kpaw, kpaw . . . *WAR* . . . ready?" "Yes, war ready!"
And all that shooting began, make-believe shooting, mashing

up our bamboo people in their bamboo beds. Then Auntie Vic
would shout, "Get out of here, boys!" Today, here we are, all

of us now women with husbands, men with wives and children,
living in London, Manchester, waiting on the war in Abidjan,

Accra, Kalamazoo, oh, Kalamazoo, Chicago, New York, Jersey
City. Now, Monrovia's on fire, kpaw, kpaw, kpaw. "Stop that

noise, boys, get out of here," Mama would scream when those
boys broke through her room, hiding right under Mama's bed.

Requiem for Auntie

When the dead first arrive in death, their eyes stand
naked and wide and bare to the bone. This gaze

numbed my girl eyes the day they brought my Auntie
home. As the dead in the land of the living made a big

fuss to welcome her, I rushed out of bed in sleeping
gown, no slippers, into the parlor I ran behind my

father, carrying white sheets for her. Up the cold
dew-wet stairs, I ran. They are keeping her upstairs

in our unfinished upper floor, I thought, to wait
for the funeral car. I could feel the cold night

shadows creeping. My stepmother's muffled
sobs up there, something gone wrong, in the dark

where my father tiptoed, carrying white sheets
and the silence. There is no silence, I say, like

the silence of death, no loneliness that surpasses
the loneliness when your Auntie has left her body,

and the living are left searching for something to do.
Now the town lay halfway between sleep and death,

between Monrovia and the dark, meandering
of the Mesurado, whose tireless going and coming

leaves one empty of words, leaves the river banks
bereft. You can hear the Mesurado going to the ocean,

and then returning. That fruitless rushing of a river. •
My Auntie laid out upon a blue mattress in the parlor

of newly laid concrete tiles, a dim lamp burning
over her head. She must not feel the cold tiles against

her skin, I imagined, but we know that the dead cannot
feel, that their skin loses its feeling at the departure

of the soul. I watched my father's fruitless making
of the bed, laying his youngest sister down, though

wide-eyed, she stared. What is she looking at, I
wanted to ask someone. What is it that the dead see,

that the living cannot know? My father stood there like
a wet bird standing in the stillness of shallow water.

The mysteries of this world are not in the living.
The mysteries of this world are in the dead cold of

death, in the weathered things of this world, in
the silence that the dead refuse to take along when

the dead leave. I saw my stepmother rush to shut those
eyes, pressing closed my Auntie's eyelids. You could still see

the thin line where her eye-liner was now a birthmark.
My stepmother went from one leg to the other, stretching

my Auntie's legs, her still polished toenails, stretching
out my Auntie's arms. There used to be Sundays when

she had come walking down that road, bringing gifts
under her arms for us children, and we'd run to meet

her partway. Today, only a nylon gown shivered around
my skin, my teeth rattling. My stepmother stood now,

wiping the water running down her own cheeks, then
breaking out wailing loud, *po-po-wlee-oh,* the Grebo cry,

and yet I stood there, two o'clock, the neighborhood asleep.
What if my Auntie had died at noon or at dusk, bringing

in the evening's hurried feet and cars, with Monrovia
hollering for her? Me, standing there, the cold dew

stairway, the sleeping houses, the swamp and the river—
so many real people at rest in an unreal country.

Today Is Already Too Much

The pigs are squealing now.
It is feeding time, and here, the younger
climb upon the older—the slob of grains
and chicken greens, rotten tomatoes
and clover grass will fatten them sadly.

The Mesurado's tide comes rushing in,
but the swamp hurriedly gulps down
all that salty water in mouthfuls—tomorrow
the river will return with
better fish and crab from the Atlantic.

Before the swamp, the hill heaves gulps of air,
breathing in today—who knows
if tomorrow will ever come.
My neighbor next door lives day to day,
to market today for bitter balls and rice,
again, to market, tomorrow.
Today, she says, is already too much.

There is wailing outside my backyard.
"Junior is drowned," I hear.
Junior has swallowed up the Mesurado
in huge gulps, and now, they are bringing in
my neighbor's boy with the afternoon tide.

I rush outdoors, barefoot down the hill.
You mean, that skinny, dark-skinned Junior
was gone fishing where the Mesurado
washes over quick swamp, quick sand?
My neighbor's boy, gulped down
all that swamp?

Right in the middle we form a circle where
death has stretched Junior out, on the ground
like a sheet. "Where did all that water settle?"
someone asked. The boy, flattened
by dark, quick swamp, not a drop
of water for all his thirst and hunger.

For Marie Antoinette

The day I discovered Marie Antoinette, she was
already dead. A woman, still clinging to her body
without the rest of her. Her stilled self, like a goddess
without her angels. Her executioners behind some
wall, on their knees, without a priest to carry

their confessions to God, to wipe the bloodstain
off their own hands. I was a hard-willed African girl
then; at fourteen, I'd just discovered I was also woman,
like you, Marie, the dead woman with my name,
crucified for what unpardonable sins, I could not say.

Was this to save your angels from dying, to annihilate
a certain past or present or future? Marie Antoinette,
slashed by revolution? I wept—it was not fair. How
many times does a fourteen-year-old discover her own
queen like this? Turning the book's pages backwards,

I wanted to know why anyone would kill a queen
the way they'd killed their queen. I held the big book
with shaky hands. That huge book, held together by
the cruel hands of history. The world pressed together
between sheets and ink and the mob, killing a queen.

What did you know, Marie? What did you care about
the rule of men? After all, you were just woman,
a stay-at-home queen, while your husband squandered
the money, bought himself more concubines,
bluffed about how many beautiful women he could

get because he was king. I wept, sitting on the bare
floor of my father's parlor, weeping for a woman
dead so many years, even the pages were beginning
to decay. I searched the book for your husband's
concubines who didn't have to go with him.

How fortunate to be a concubine, to be the other
woman who didn't have to carry the world's guilt to
the gallows. The look on their faces, those pretty French
girls, their half smiles and grins, their tearless cheeks,
and how lucky to be left outside history like this.

Two

In the Beginning

In the beginning, there were women, and all things,
creeping and non-creeping, were good.

That was before time could tell daylight from night.
When men could speak women's tongues; before

the sea turned blue and took up rolling, foaming, like
a big glass of fresh palm wine. Before oceans learned

to rise and fall, before rivers were first named *rivers*.
Before they named the Cavalla River, *Cavalla*, after

the fish or the fish after the town, or the town after
the river. When Cape Palmas, where I come from,

became *Cape Palmas;* before there was even a cape
or palm trees. Before Cape Palmas began to give birth

to palm trees that sprouted with fat bottoms and began
to rise, and the coconut learned to be sister to the nut

palm, and the nut palm to the bamboo palm, the bamboo
palm to the thatch; or when their grandfather made

them blood relations or straw relations or bamboo
relations or cabbage relations or long, thin leaves

relations, or whatever it is that makes them seem
identical twins. But bamboo knows how to prick my

finger when I touch it with an angry heart; the palm tree
will prick lightly, while the coconut stands there, tall.

Coconut breasts hanging from its chest, or head,
or whatever. The way a bamboo grove used to prick

our toes when Mudi and I wandered under its swampy
territory. That was before the time when women took

upon themselves to birth babies, even though men
knew how to, or before men went around boasting

of having this many children and this many sons upon
their mere fingers. *Iyeeh* says men really birthed babies

then, and women boasted of being the fathers of babies
then, and the children ran for their fathers like they do

today for their mothers when a father calls them for
whipping with a cane. That was long before the car road

bulldozed the giant walnut, the oak, chopping up
the towns and the forests into roads, and rubber trees

sprang up where the forests were, and the coffee
became a tree, becoming first cousin to the cocoa,

and the palm nuts went to the city to be sold for coins.
We girls grew wings like pepper birds—no, no, like

eagles, or like jet planes, and could fly or hop on a truck
to the city where streetlights cannot tell the villager

from the city dweller; where a man cannot tell his wife
from his lover; his *inside* children from his *outside*

children; where all have lost their hearts to the bars
and the dangling lights, and people fight on street corners;

and after all that, I and all the girls of the world learned
to run wild too, like wild flowers—no, no, wild, like men.

All the women of the world becoming just men.

This Is What I Tell My Daughter

If my father hadn't scared me, I wouldn't be here.
I'd be somewhere down Jallah Town or Slip Way,
where the Mesurado dumps its junk by dark swamps.
I'd be carrying buckets full of dirt to turn
Monrovia's swamps into dry land. Or I'd be
somebody's wife, trying to be somebody's wife.
This is how I scare my daughter.

You wouldn't be here. You'd be somewhere,
where babies wait in long lines to be born,
little babies with sore feet, waiting
in the unborn world, where food can't grow.
I would have had ten children before you were born.
You, there, standing in line, waiting to be born,
while I'd be in some overcrowded town,
some unknown city or village, with skinny-
legged children, mucus noses, bare feet,

crying for food. I'd be there, one husband
each month, one room each month.
On Capitol Bye Pass, where I grew up,
all the boys knew how to get a girl pregnant.
All sorts of men and boys, all sorts of people
lurking at windows, in doorways.
Plenty of men from Nigeria, from Sudan,
from far away villages in Liberia, from Mars.
This is what I tell my daughter.

My father, a barbed-wire fence,
his needle-poking eyes, scaring boys away.
The boys called him "CIA chief."
The girls on Capitol Bye Pass—with their perky,
brown cheeks, their smooth pretty skin,
their sophisticated steps.

My father called them *gronna-girls,*
bringing home sad trophies in teen arms.

War Baby

Ma Hawa sent for me because Gbayon
swallowed his breath with a piece of candy.
It stuck to his three-year-old throat and took
his breath down with it. Our neighbor's son lay
still and pale, no fingers or toes or eyelids moving,
yet, in the weeds about the house, the wind tossed
things about, aside, and neighbors hollered and scrambled
to bring the boy back. Someone whispered that they
would have a long way to go, to get to Gbayon's father
who had gone to war all these years.
In all the whispers, Gbayon's mother screamed to keep
her wailing above the gossip.
Gbayon's father was standing right there, hearing it all;
that someone would have to cross a river to get
Gbayon's father. If the birds should hear this,
we will have a long night on our hands, I thought,
a long night on our hands. It takes a real woman to know
who her baby's father is, and not tell. To stand up
to a warrior husband and tell him that the child dying
was conceived out of season, out of house, out of the usual
way of things, and say to another man,
this is your child indeed, your child. This child that
was now one relic of our war. When all the *real* men
had left for war, and the women, left behind
to watch the rockets fall, to watch the children die
of kwashiorkor, of measles, to watch it all go up
in smoke, and then in the quiet, right when it was
too cold to wait, commandos took the women
in the early mornings and evenings, the bloodless
part of the civil war, now becoming bloody.
On the ground, the dying boy twitched, a toe twitched,
a finger moved. It was not good for a war child
to leave in such a way, you know.

The Moon Poem

In Monrovia, my mother will walk outdoors tonight
under this same blue light beneath which her children

ran wild. Today, the old moon hunches against
the dark sky, having gathered wood for the sun's bonfire

in the sky tomorrow. In Tugbakeh, we grew up trampling
grass from one goal pole to the other, our football field

always ready for players' feet to do their dancing upon
the green grass. In the goal, did the goalkeeper pray

this flying ball would fly away over the pole, in the clouds,
forever? We chased boys under hibiscus bushes as the ball

grew wings. Hide and seek, we ran, not knowing why a boy
chases a girl. In Tugbakeh, hibiscus hedges cut us off from

the town, from the world, from football fans, yelling at an
antique ball. Under the moonlight, we girls lined up,

the moon and the bluff boys and our shadows, chasing. We
stopped, and ahh, the moon and those green, Tugbakeh boys

gathered shadows around us. The football flying, the crowd
cheering, the girls and boys, dancing, the moon waiting.

They Want to Rise Up

In the unknown hours, when daylight is coming in,
and the dark gathers for departure,
when the winds stir pebbles along Liberia's shores,
you can hear the wailing.
From the coast of Harper to Sinoe, from Sinoe
to Bassa, from the coast of Bassa to Monrovia,
from Monrovia to Robertsport.

The ocean begins its soft whistling, like a new widow
that first morning after her loss.
All the dead at the ocean's bottom, whose bones
still search for refuge.
From the Atlantic's bed, a song rises in the ocean currents.
It is their sound that comes and goes, at dawn,
when the night is splintered into invisible bits.

Elegy to West Point Fishermen

Your corrugated zinc shacks leaned into one another,
like a mask of crocodile scales, along

the fevered Atlantic, where waves wash away
white sand, tirelessly rising, falling, rolling, slapping.

We said your town would someday crumble
into this ocean; you'd die in the Mesurado,

just ahead. *One day these fishermen will all drown
in their sleep.* But you did not drown,

and your charcoal grills did not set your shacks ablaze . . .
you'd come too far to kill yourselves so ordinarily.

But one day the sand pulled you back as you tried to flee.
Before you'd had time to gather your fishing nets,

your canoes, waiting for the slap of water, your smokers,
ready to smoke *gbapleh* and snappers thin.

Will your bony fish graze these shanty skies smoky again?
Monrovia's skies exploded with jets, and you

exploded too, all of you, children, mothers, fathers,
fishermen, the smell of fish now your gravestones.

Three

Coming Home to *Iyeeh*

I'm coming home so *Iyeeh* will die. So many years away,
and now, suitcases loaded with rolls of black cotton fabric,
matching earrings and hats. Second Mourning dresses
with lace trimmings at sleeves and collars, black and white
lilies running down all over. White laces at the hems
to bring out all that black.

This mourning must be properly done.

Some purple skirts and blouses, a purple dress to aid
in Second Mourning. I will need matching black shoes,
two-inch heels or just flats—even though I'm not one for flats
or rather, flats are not for me—*Iyeeh* will not want anyone
taking up her time and her funeral or wake-keeping uselessly
fretting over their own knees or joints, shoes or heels.

Every teardrop falling, every dirge sung, every wail or moan
or sigh . . . all the drumming and praise songs must be hers.
Iyeeh, Mother, *Khadi Wheh, Wahnjeh,* we praise you—
it is your children who now praise you . . . your wandering
stranger-children now coming home.
Where there are trumpets, they will sound.
We do not pour libation with ancestral hands or gourds.

They are the ones who drink libation . . . it is we who must pour.
All these years, the ground was parched and cracked.
Years of sun without rain or a bucket of water. I'm coming home
at last . . . the owl perches high at night, but the rooster sits low
on a cocoa branch. When the owl flies away at dawn
from the oak, it is the rooster, crowing, so the sun will rise.

The child that wanders comes home only to graves.

A Dirge for Charles Taylor

Charles Taylor sits like a wasted child
who has smashed the sacred bowl.
Firestarter of the hushed town,
Ghankay, the leopard
who came to town at harvest, eating
both the harvester and the harvest.
We will find our way back home by the imprints
of your bloody claws, *Ghankay.*
Banquet tickets to celebrate your dying
have sold out, but you will not die.
Plunderer, destroyer, do we delight
in your plundering or do we lament
abroad in other people's countries?
We have forgotten how
to sing the dirges you taught us to sing.
Those who die abroad now send their spirits
by boats, wading the deep waters at night
just to get back home.
Should we tell our children that there was
once Monrovia, sitting on a hill
where steel rocks breathed out hot vapors,
inhaling moist air? Should we tell our daughters
that there was a place where one could
put a shack down and stay alive on dry rice,
red palm oil and rumors?

Around the Mountains

Sandy winds her car around little mountains
from Buffalo to Olean while we talk of husbands,

children, and the years. We're in a maze, these
Alleghenies humping, chasing one another up

and down. They will take you, if you please, until
the skies fall asleep in your eyes. Now I can see

how the hills lose us or how our eyes lose the hills,
giving up so the skies can take possession,

like a teacher of my child. Sandy says when
we get over the mountains the sun will meet us

down below. Sometimes it is forever before we get
over the mountain, and the sun comes out

in trickling twilight. Sandy says when the trees
come out, this place is a paradise, but this year

the snow was forever falling. When the trees
come out, tell the trees, Sandy, to make the flowers

white and purple; to mourn the life, lost, the laughter
in Monrovia's streets, of people in the market places

and on the long beaches; to mourn my neighbors
who wanted to know who you were, Sandy,

my American friend. Eleven years, and here we are,
chasing the Alleghenies, bargaining with these

hills and cops along roadside exits. Sandy says
she was afraid we'd all been killed, and I tell of how

a missile landed on our back porch, where Sandy
had stood, sparklers in hand, singing to America

on the Fourth of July; another missile bursting through
concrete walls, landing in the room where she

and Barbara used to sleep, the room my children
called Sandy and Barbara's room. I tell of leaving

home and refugee camp, of coming to America,
and Sandy sighs. But here I am, after eight years,

I'm going to St. Bonaventure to read poetry, where
Matt is Sandy's three-year-old, and Paul, her husband.

Paul, such a strong name for a husband, Sandy.
I'm going to read poetry where St. Bonaventure

University spreads itself thin on a field taken captive
by the Alleghenies, where students fall in love not

with the Alleghenies, as I have, but with each other.
I like my flowers spread out in colorful petals, a bed

under the skies. We know that spring is just
for a season. I like my husband warm, where summer

is eternal, when his eyes are laughing, and their pupils
fold under the milk in his eyes. I want to fold me

under my husband's arms, under his breath, the way
we did in the 1980s, before the war, before the children

came, before my strands of hair began to give way to
lost years, before the rebels came, before the soldiers,

before our years were ambushed into memory.

Elegy for Dessie

My telephone rang in the news at half past ten.
Your news arriving through a cordless phone.
The day outside my window came in, uninvited.
Snowflakes sparkling, falling
in silver pieces here in Kalamazoo.
Such an uncommitted day it was, Dessie.
January is not the time to die here in America.

In Monrovia, we would have marched you
in the Harmattan winds. Moist air from the Atlantic,
sweeping grave dirt away so
you could go down. Now all over America, telephones
must be ringing in the news
that Dessie Webster has just died.

Will a friend somewhere pick up the phone
today in Monrovia, London, Accra, Abidjan, Sinoe,
and break the news to some man or woman
and run to tell someone, human answering machines
holding the news for us all? All over the world,
your friends will have to make way for you now,
to hold up an hour for you now.

I stood there, at the window after that cruel phone call,
thinking of you in college. Everyone used
to talk about you as if you were the legend
for younger girls to live. They say it was New York
that killed you. That you must have wandered into
its glitter at night and lost your own glitter—
all your innocence and faith, gone.
Friends who used to love you no longer

loved you after that. Isn't that something, Dessie?
When you called last October to tell us that
you were going to die soon, apologizing for dying on us,
and Mlen-Too, beside me on the couch, held on
to the other phone while I begged you not to die,
Jesus, how does a woman like you die?
You who knew how to take life unawares?

Remember how you sent for us in 1993
so we could see where you lived, in Queens?
Your car slipping in and out of the Manhattan
traffic as though you owned the streets and the city?
As though you created the city with your own hands?
On Saturday, I saw you rise at dawn and set
the house smoking with home cooking—

palm butter and rice, cassava and gravy, fufu and soup,
chicken, fried deep and hot. One moment,
you were laughing; one moment, you were banging
pots and dishes. At noon, there were your guests—
old friends from back home, new New Yorkers,
sitting and talking in your backyard

as if they truly loved you. Maybe they truly
loved you, Dessie. I stood at your upstairs window
each day at dawn to see your city, to watch
your town rise with the speed of a jet.
If I could know New York, I would know you,
I told myself. Did you bring us over
to New York so we could keep you forever?

Transfiguration

From the plane I see skyscrapers like needles.
Train tracks winding up huge towns like thread
knotted in between so the needle stays in place.

If the needle falls out, it may prick someone's foot, I think,
or turn to mere rust. There goes the lake
I used to love, becoming like spilled water wending its

way to the carpet of lawns below.
And then the plane jerks and rocks; potholes in the sky
are making their presence felt. We hit a rock,

a bump, we're flying above little knots of unknown people
in unknown towns. My mother used to say,
There is nothing to boast of in this life, my child, nothing.
From dust, we will all return to mere dust, she said, when
suddenly I could take on wings, carried away with myself.

When I Meet Moses

Forty years, and already, the body is ready to go.
Knuckles ache, fingers fail you, and your eyes see things

that aren't even there. At night, your ears are like crickets
in your backyard, ringing in midnight before midnight.

When your joints crack, it's like an old door creaking
at dawn, when the baby's asleep, and you tell yourself,

"In the morning, I'll oil that creaking door; I'll oil
that door." All the hinges holding you together cry out,

it's time to leave now, although the party's just started.
Now, it's not just your teenage daughter disobeying.

When you were twenty, you were like a spring; the bright,
funny, long eye-lashed girl; face as smooth as a newborn's.

It was your big *tumba,* balanced hip and hairy legs
announcing your arrival, and all eyes turned. Now, see

all these signals each year brings—sagging flesh, painful
joints. Didn't we girls think our mothers would be the last

with aching knees? When I meet Moses, I'll let him say
how he lived over one hundred long years, already past

eighty before seeing the Burning Bush that I see everyday.
Needing a cane only to stretch over some body of water

that splits in two, after going back and forth between God
and Pharaoh and those stubborn people below

that mountain. What kind of knees will carry a man, already
long past a hundred, up and down a mountain, carrying

the Ten Commandments engraved on stone? Now at forty,
why is my body in such a big hurry to be rid of me?

For Robert Frost

They say you used to hear voices.
Your mother heard voices.
Your sister heard voices.
So they locked her up in an asylum—
put a padlock over all that poetry
forever. I hear voices too, like you,
Robert. I hear my children in the
kitchen, banging cups and dishes,
clanging glasses above their screaming.

Eating at home is such a task now.
I hear them throwing pillows, winding
through narrow passageways.
My mother said they will someday
grow up and leave home. They will
still have limbs and eyes and teeth
when they are twenty. When they
are thirty, they will take on the world
with bare claws. Where you must

have mixed fresh chicken manure
with thin lines of a poem, I surrender
to a child's lingering cry. You must
have sat upon a tree stump, chicken
manure riding air bubbles about you
in the middle of a poem after apple
picking. Winter breeze in the woods,
captured by the absoluteness

of subsistence farming. How does
a rooster get its feeding in the middle
of a poem, Robert? Can a hen
hatch its eggs beneath a poem's mood?

The Corrupt Shall Rise Incorruptible

It's going to be something to see, right after
I'm dead and gone. Uncontrolled laughing down
the hall where my body lies in state,
and everyone turns to see if it's me getting up
to look over things, the way I have,
sending a peaceful room bubbling—
those secret enemies filing out so I can fill the room
with all my imperfection.

My three-week-old laundry out in some
dark closet, shoved there by my sister, Nanu,
who hates doing her own laundry anyway,
hates taking charge of things after anyone is dead.
All my friends looking so grim in this room
where silence has taken over without disturbing
a speck of dirt. All my loud laughing, now

immortalized, my fear of house cleaning,
immortalized; yelling at *deaf children,* over,
and done. And the dishes—let's get down
to the bottom of dirty dishes—palm oil stains glow
on imitation china; fufu, cooked before I died,
its residue, sticky, the way gum sticks
between the teeth of a grouchy Kru woman
awaiting her uncommitted lover's arrival
for the Christmas eve dance.

Parched crust from rice cooked in my dying hour,
in the sink, exploding, as if to wail for me,
to mourn my passing, even though I almost never did
any dishes in my lifetime. Has grief so changed
the way of things that people actually think
I used to be clean?
It's going to be something to see—

my still naughty brother attempting to have
my dirty pots, laundry, and dusty carpet follow me
to the bottom of the grave. So when I rise
at the trumpet's last call, there will be chores for me
before I'm caught up in the air. And Jesus,
let's talk about Jesus, standing at the top
of Jacob's ladder.

That same ladder in Jacob's dream,
after he'd duped Esau out of Esau's birthright.
All that blessing just for one tasteless, spicy,
bowl of alligator soup and palm oil on rice. Okay, maybe
not alligator soup, some soup, and Esau, the hungry fool,
Jacob, the trickster, now fleeing on foot,
Mama's boy, a rotten business—

that crooked business deal, still haunting us today.
Angels, descending, African angels, black wings,
climbing, descending, climbing,
and Jesus in a Total Involvement Suit,
long black beard, big brown eyes, wide open arms,
telling me to move my bed into any house
here in Heaven.

Right down Nile Street in Heaven, I pick a house
where I sit, my palm under my chin, to worry
about my grandchildren not feeding their children well,
my great-grandchildren who cannot make up their beds.
My great-great-grand, not polite to an old woman
in the supermarket's aisles, not signing the cross
at the mention of my dear old name.

Jesus saying, "Forget the dishes, forget
the carpet cleaning and the dusting, forget
that your children must raise their own children,
forget the friends who haven't missed you all that much;
that the day you died, babies were born.

Forget that old woman in the supermarket aisles.
Forget that you forgot you are not God."

We've Done It All

In my family, all the wars have been fought,
battles, won. All the losers have long settled
their losses in cattle or goats and sheep,
in women or farmlands or out of town.
Like *Bai* packing up, a tiny bundle under
now failing arms, leaving us even though
his eyes cannot see beyond a gaze. He's been
here so long, the Old Man no longer
needs eyes, no longer needs feet, no longer
needs us. Today, we watch him walk out
to Borbor Naapoh's farm when Borbor Tugba

says something he will not take; then again,
packing for Borbor Tugba's farm when
Borbor Naapoh says something he will not take.
In the dark night, just before bed when in
the rubber bush, you can hear crickets chipping
the evening into bits of darkness, fireflies
rush to bring him their own portable flashlights
as *Bai* stumbles out to leave, walking
miles of darkness to his younger son; or as
we look in the dark and see him hobble
into the house, out of the cold. As a child,

I wondered how old one gets before one loses
all fear of darkness, all fear of family feuds
or reasoning? How one sets one son loose just
to bind another. A distant cousin is sent away
for incest—whipped, peppered, and sent away from
Tugbakeh, where it is home to him, and never
again will be seen by family or friends
or that cousin he had raped.

The World in Long Lines

We are comforted by the breeze from the Atlantic
carrying salty, moist waves upon its shoulders.

Strong winds from the shores of Harper bring us
a day's consolation. Especially when the sun in March

parches the whole earth dry. It is that time of year again,
the wind blows hard; trees sway on their buttocks, dust

flies for freedom, and an old lady somewhere on a rice
field near Harper pulls wet weeds with rough, wet hands.

Farming was never meant to be easy. She takes in deep
breaths of salty air, like the child upon its mother's back.

The wind's audacity is out of control, reaching doorways,
passing through uninviting halls, then outdoors where

freedom has no strings attached. We too, our audacity
seems out of control; one man to three wives; too many

mouths to feed. The old lady wants to go down to her
grave knowing her grandchildren will be fed. Is she

afraid to leave us in charge of her earth? The suffering
in this world will overwhelm us someday. Should God

one day hand over all this world's wealth to the poor
out there in India, Nigeria, Liberia, China, Russia,

down the street from me—the world, standing in long
lines, waiting to turn the old rich into poor beggars?

All the Soft Things of Earth

All the soft things of earth sighed when my mother died.
All the quiet noises of this world stopped, at once.

Not even the drying, wet leaves, after fall had tossed
them so. Not even the robin that sits upon a twig

in my backyard knew what to say when my mother died.
Not even wet tears which death demands. All the soft

crevasses of this earth and of ground, sighed; the dent
crevasses of pavement after so many years. All the hands

that tremble at bewilderment, my hands lie helpless
and cold on my lap. When the wind blew past, it sighed

deep, like taking in deep breaths of air, a laboring,
as if the universe had just stopped. As if I had just died.

Becoming Ebony

"Did I come all the way here to hide from the sun?"
Mama would sigh. I can still see Mama standing

at the window, watching dark clouds, cold winds,
yellow leaves—November. Leaves from

my neighbor's yard arrive from yesterday's fall.
November rations its sunshine here in Michigan.

Today, I wish the end of clouds, the end of sky, the end
of windows—only curtains bright with daffodils,

African violets, hibiscus, wild thorny roses side by side.
I want to see the end of neighbors with falling maple

leaves, a lazy dog on a leash, barking at flying leaves.
Those who have no windows do not wait for the sun

to come in. Those who have no windows will not hear
my neighbor's dog. Here in my living room, the glass

window bends the sunlight; a dying fern leans. I am
a killer of plants seeking refuge in my living room.

I want to see the end of death. An ebony lion on my
glass table waits patiently for the sun, like Mama,

in Byron Center, waiting at the window for the sun
to come in, waiting for the war to end at home.

The day Mama died, I waited at the window to see
if the sun would come in, to see if my brother would

call again—the uncertainty of waiting so a moment will
undo itself, to undo that dreaded call, to undo death.

How many calls can undo death? An ebony carving
knows the uncertainty of skin, the uncertainty of time,

the uncertainty of waiting. Brown wood, darkening
slowly, becoming ebony all the way through.

The ebony at home knows how to unfurl wide, green
branches, how to die slowly, becoming woodwork,

a ritual mask for the harvest dance, an ebony lion,
perhaps, on a glass table. That familiar feel of carving

knife, the sharp cut, when the carver no longer recalls
his purpose. Crooked edges, polished by the artist's

rough hands, and then, what was wood becomes marble—
a raw tree trunk yielding its life until what was wood

becomes iron. The ebony knows how brief color is—
when sap licks itself dry into rough threads of wood.

They say after the sap is gone, then comes strength.
The ebony knows how final color is, how final death is.

Four

For My Husband

We lived through rationed minutes at Soul Clinic
Mission displaced center, on rationed grains and fear,

and then night visited its shadows despite the odorous
air from the Killing Rubber Bush. One day I asked

if you were sure this was still Liberia. You looked
at me and said, "It's okay, my wife, it's okay."

Our children, ill, and starving, pleading for milk, for
a candy bar, for bread and meat, for a birthday gift

and cake, and we looked at each other, and sighed,
knowing what children do not know. There were

no mirrors, no wardrobes, no saloons where we girls
knew how to spend a whole day, braiding or relaxing

long, dark hair, amidst the chattering room of girls,
working my long dark hair so I could let it loose

the way I used to let it loose. How I used to twist
and turn for you to see my new hairdo. Now with

no shaving blades or perfume soap, no perfumes
or nail polish, no iron or clothes to iron. Today you

looked at me, and said how beautiful I had become
in the war. And when the night came, we fell asleep

listening to shooting outside. You said you loved me
even though you saw what I did not see. And sitting

in the crowded camp, we held hands tight, waiting,
praying. I said I loved you while I saw what you did

not see. All the bones of our jaws and chests, piercing
through flabby flesh. We had become bones, eyes

and skin, but we did not know, and didn't wish to know.
I had lost my lipstick or couldn't recall if I had ever

had lipstick. And when we ate cooked green papayas
for potatoes, the heart of palm trees for meat, craw-craw

crabs for seafood, we shut our eyes tight, laughing
at ourselves. We were the lucky ones with no mirrors

in the war. Were we the lucky ones with eyes to see
the smoke, to see the missiles flying towards what used

to be home, breathing in air from the dead? We waited
to see if the food would kill us before the rebels could

kill us. We ate leaves we did not know we could eat;
we ate anyway, and lived through eating. We tried this

or that to see if we would not die eating this or that.
We made laughter we did not know we had. Did we

learn to sleep on cold floors, laughing at ourselves over
and over, our new eating habits, our new bathing habits,

our new songs, days handed to us in brief interrupted
installments? We were becoming new people, we told

ourselves. At night, we went to sleep knowing how far
away tomorrow was. Often, I looked to see if you'd

catch me smiling the way I caught you smiling.

50

Wandering Child

The child that wanders will not know her mother's grave.
—Grebo proverb

In my father's house it is payday, just before Christmas,
so the house bubbles full of unwelcome guests—

It is so long ago now—twenty years? Maybe, thirty.
There is beer, hot-pepper-soup and laughter.
Pay day, my father is making pay-day talk.
In the kitchen, my father's wife, Ma Nmano, is cooking
goat meat soup with crushed tomatoes in a huge pot;
or we children are cooking the soup while
Ma sits there like the traffic police, pointing to this
or that as we rush around to give her what she needs.

Eight years ago at the airport, it is my own mother
standing there, wiping tears not just from the war.
She wipes one drop and then another while the plane
groans and waits so my family and I can flee home.
Ma Nmano is here too, wailing not just for my departure,
but also for TK, my foster brother.

TK who had promised her a nice bronze coffin, a long,
white gown to wear so when she met God, he'd know
she was Hne Nmano, *Sagba,* and nothing less.
TK and I would hold a great wake-keeping,
lots of food and lots of talk . . .
for our childless mother, and I'd sit there on The Mat
with my hair open, tearful, wailing,

a red mourning band around my head.
All the Grebo people would line up to shake my hand,
long faces; the women would sit close to me,
arms around my shoulders. Then on funeral day,

the Grebo band would arrive, playing,
"Na Nyebioh, Nyankeh Hne, Na Nyebioh."
Then we'd dance the way she would dance during those

New Year's Day mornings when the bands
came with the new year to wake us.
New Year's Day, and we children ran out to the front
and rocked to Grebo rhythms. And all the last minute
fuss in the kitchen, whether to cook palm butter
in this huge pot or potato greens in that.
The women arguing among themselves over

how much pepper the wailing women would want,
and the kola nut bowl there in the middle of it all;
people coming in, taking a bite of kola nut
and a pinch of hot spicy pepper. The beer and gin
and soft drinks passed around while TK
and my brother, Toh, ran up and down, checking on
the grave site, or whether there was enough

for everyone to eat and drink. Grandchildren
she never really had, running around playing *Nafoot,*
mimicking the wailing women on The Mat,
while the neighborhood filled with hundreds of wanted
and unwanted mourners. Family from all over would
come back home, sleeping everywhere in the house
because it was time to send Ma off. Instead,

one day rebels came for TK, shot him right there,
my father and Ma, pleading . . . Here I am, peeling eggplant.
My childhood follows me around where I slice
one eggplant after the other, to fry and steam cook.
I will cook make-believe Liberian Torgborgee.
They say Africans want to have Africa in America,

pounding fufu to swallow, hunting for cow's feet in
Chicago, Detroit, or New York. A hundred miles in search
of palm oil, gari, palm butter, sweet potato leaves.
Every alien wants to find home in other people's country.
After I fled the war, Ma died. One month, my father waited
for everyone who couldn't come to put The Mat down.

Small Desires

We had become small desires—a few cups of rice
to feed a family of ten; no salt or sugar, no oil
or beans, just a few pounds of raw, white rice
to feed those who might be dead tomorrow.
Refugees desiring a place to wait and take in
small air. If you ask me about the mother
awakened by tomorrow's needs at two

in the morning, I'd say, *the ceiling is her company*
and the crickets outdoors. Her children are asleep
while the old clock ticks hard; about the house,
silence has a voice. As the woman lies still in bed,
is she content to have a bed? No bombing, no shooting?
The poor of this world have small desires—
a loaf of bread, a pound of rice, a few small fish,

food for today, a few tablets to heal an ailing child,
fresh water to drink, a spot to lay the head.
The baby Jesus was laid on a bed of odorous hay.
Small wishes don't have to have legs or arms,
just the heart's soft beats. Three children, my husband,
and I are clinging to one small suitcase after the war.
We are standing at O'Hare amidst suitcases banging,
it is Welcome-to-America day.

To be alive still is such a matter for dancing.
Dan Denk is here at O'Hare with jackets, boots, hugs, tears—
All our years before the war come rushing amidst
this airport, and my eyes refuse to look on the years
in my eyes. To have a friend like Daniel Denk,
standing here, and a place to hide now is all
there is to this life, and then tomorrow is settled.

There are a few things civil war can teach—to eat
the nonedibles of this life, wild crabs, green papayas
in place of bread, bamboo shoots for fish,
beans as if beans were potatoes. Displacement is not
a matter of will. Finding a place to hide is reason
for dancing, no shouting. Those who must hide
cannot give away their hiding place.

When I Rise to Look the Sunshine in Its Bare Eye

Today settles at dawn, taking over my collar bones,
moving down my upper back, my spine,
back and forth, the pain travels.
Molecules of migraine tighten muscles to make
room for the afternoon sunshine, a waiting place
as the day passes by. The plans of today become
like mountains gathering store upon my head.
Bed covers huddle or I huddle against bed covers,

but my husband may never know how memory eats
away the day while I still lie in bed. I have no reason
though, to fear the day. A single day has never
before conquered me; not even when bombs fell
at my back yard. When I rise to look the sunshine
in its bare eye, my mind travels from here to Liberia,
where war has snapped away the years from us all.

The BBC news says that my old neighborhood is now
a *Beverly Hills* in Monrovia, in a now bleak country.
Charles Taylor has taken over Congo Town
with his rebels, our *Warrior Master* as though he were
the British Crown partitioning Africa at the dinner
table, handing out a huge continent in small rations.
Charles Taylor has settled in, now all the women
are concubines. All the girls are become mistresses

before puberty. Where are the men? You will find them
walking the streets, seeking work. Someone told them
war is over. The men are become concubines.
All of us are now concubines of war. I sit here
in Kalamazoo, the snow falls in small flakes,
the ground turns from green grass to white.
My new life is becoming a sofa that will not let me

recall how I fled from home from the war.
Now all the years have become for me a longing
to go back home, a waiting to return, to slip back home
and see what the country I still love has become.

A Poem for My Father

Pa wants another degree from me, a PhD,
for sure. Me, his oldest girl child who was supposed
to be a man. As if God won't let Pa into Heaven
without a family PhD. Won't listen to Pa's
old arguments about too many children plus too many
hungry relatives to feed. Too many Mats to put down,
and all those relatives from Kaluway arriving, red with
dust from two days' dusty highway. Heavy loads of palm
nuts, red palm oil, bags of cassavas, potatoes, eddoes . . .

all that rice, pounded so white, you can see right
through each grain. You see, we all know how that rice
was pounded just for each trip. Relatives, coming with dried
bush meat, smoked dry, like a rock. All those loads
of food, coming to our door at dawn, a truck's old engine,
beating leaded gasoline to help pollute our already
polluted earth. The cost of bringing all that foodstuff
through five hundred miles of rocky, hilly, country roads

of Grand Gedeh, Nimba, Bong . . . all this trouble for
nothing, since the loads are for some other relatives who
cannot afford to pay the truck driver's fare.
But Pa is the town's big book man—pays everyone's debt,
marries up everyone's daughter, and when they die,
Pa pays the grave digger, the dirge singer, puts the bronze
on every casket, the black on every *lappa,* gin
for the mourning table, feeds the women on The Mat,
so the burial is merry, and the dead stand proud.

Pa buys the kola nuts to chew, meats up the soup,
so The Mat goes wild. That's why I'm back in school
after all these years. In all the homesickness and the snow,
Pa says, "Get that PhD before I die—
before they lay me in this earth." If I don't, the ground

beneath my feet will rock; my feet will slip and slide under
my father's turning over and over in his soggy grave.
The whole earth will open under my feet, a house
or two may tumble, rock, and fall . . . the ground,
opening its wide mouth to swallow me up.

In This Town

In this town
the Presbyterian church spreads its wings like a jumbo jet.
Sprawled upon the street corner,
larger than the town.
Houses sporadically dropped
here and there,
in between overgrown brushes.
Gravestones beckon us motorists.
A gas station calls and we stop to inquire.
A Main Street here
and a Burdick there.
Is there a Main Street in every town
and a Burdick close to each Main?

Nothing makes sense to me
except these cattle grazing in fields in the surrounding plains.
I love these cornfields and dilapidated barns,
this emptiness and the silence.
Will there be festivals where villagers
come out, where mothers dance
the end of year goodbye,
fathers carrying *kinjas* of the river catch?
In my hometown, *Iyeeh*'s eyes water at the passing
of years, grinning at children running wild.
Will there be new brides, adorned

in beads, chalked beauty and virginity?
Buttocks swaying to drumming
as old suitors watch with envious eyes?
Does anything here make sense
with no coconut or palm fronds waving
in midair, children running barefoot,
while birds perch on tree branches, singing
songs only villagers know?

Where are the chief, the elders, and their drums?
Will there be kola nuts inside the door for me?

My Neighbors' Dogs

All my neighbors have dogs, uncountable breeds
of dogs, little leashes around their dog necks.
My neighbors train their dogs to bark at dawn
like the rooster, to rouse the whole neighborhood
out of its sleep. In the evening when
I come home from work, these yelping,
howling, overweight dogs
welcome my car from the street
into my driveway. My next-door neighbor's dog
wants to tear down our wire fence. Giant claws
and teeth, its elephant body at the fence.
Someone needs to speak to that dog.
There are people in this world
who live on dogs, who will not understand
a dog in bed, a dog on a couch, a dog yelping.
There are places in this world where
kindhearted people eat dog at dinner.
But one neighbor keeps hers under
her comforter. Another ties her dog
to our shared fence, in the rain, in snow or sleet.

My neighbor has decided to keep her dog
chained to our fence, in case the gas meter reader
misses the meter, or the prowler comes in
while we're all gone. All my neighbors share
their dogs with me. That bark at two A.M.,
when all I need is sleep. My neighbor's
poodles are on water pills. They pee all night,
and my neighbor loves it that her little sweet
poodles keep us all awake.
At my backyard, I stand in my driveway
for my other neighbor's dog to bark until
it runs out of saliva. The dog wants to tear down
the wire fence that keeps us all apart;

our common fence with nothing common
between us, its invisible line keeping us
from knowing one another.
My neighbors' dogs are so kind.
One of these days, they may eat away our fence.

A Letter to My Brother Coming to America

We just extended our daylight hours—so we can
shop the malls, pay our bills, shovel out snow,
take the garbage out. We still have twenty-four
hours in a day. I wash my own clothes,
cook my own meals, scrub my kitchen floor,
vacuum my house. Here, there are no maids
or houseboys, no long line of relatives

arriving at my door on Saturday mornings, needing
a few dollars for rice and fish, for a child's tuition.
Homesickness chips up my memories into cassava
pieces to fry at a street corner in Monrovia.

Our houses stand in silent rows here in Kalamazoo.
When I can almost hear the breeze pass, I wonder,
did a neighbor die, move away? Get a divorce?
Get married? Do they have children?
Do they not have children? Is my neighbor
white or black? Would my neighbors like me
if they knew my name? Do I have a neighbor?

Are they going to carve up your life too?

I wait at the window for the sunshine.
The pizza man will deliver my pizza, my only visitor
in months. I hear the bang when the post woman comes.
Pull a curtain, and bang, she's gone. Of course,
my friends still say, "We're getting together, someday,
we're getting together." Dear Brother, did you hear me?

I used to hug people when I first came: a cashier at
the store, my next-door neighbor, the gas meter reader,
the girl down the street. I pulled on to sleeves,
keeping track of the homeless girl downtown.
And then, I settled. Are you still planning to join me?

My New Insurance Plan

My insurance company called me today—a great new plan
that's just right for me—thousands of dollars for me when

I'm already dead and gone, in the grave, while I lie still,
clasped in soil and water, beneath stones, and cold; my

husband or my children or Uncle Sam will claim this
benefit for me. But first, I have to die a certain way, in

a certain month, let's say, December or January, when
snow piles up along street corners and sidewalks, when

drivers can't get to work in their own cars. When cars go
sliding and crashing into walls. I must not die of AIDS

or pneumonia or chest pains; heart attacks will not satisfy
this great new plan. I have to crash on the expressway, into

a wall, a school building, into a house; I must die instantly
or they'll never pay. I cannot be hooked up to machines

or call in Jack Kervorkian; my insurance plan won't cover
such a procedure as Jack's, and the police can't arrive before

I swallow my last breath. My bones, all of my bones must
be broken, but my eyes must be in place. I cannot give up any

body parts before I'm safely in the grave. The cost, the soft
pleading lady convinces is only a hundred dollars a month, a

bare hundred from my monthly paycheck, while I wait for my
car to come sliding on ice, seat belt strapped tightly around

me, buckled, of course; me, crashing into a welcoming wall.

These Are the Reasons the Living Live

Here come my children again, pushing chairs out,
in my way. They giggle, fall, and scream.
The family room leads into Ade's room
all littered with broken toys, old crayons, broken
only in the middle. Half-used paint, caked and cracked,
the treasures of a six-year-old.
These are the reasons the living live
and the dead decided to die.

My teenage daughter is laughing tonight.
You can write a poem on her foreface tonight—
let it linger in her eyes, hang a poem from a strand
of her thick, black hair.
To hold laughter in a line of a poem is like
capturing my daughter in a poem. It will be easier
to catch a bird with my left hand, easier to pull
out a lion's tooth, to hold a line of a poem down

to the level of Adam's wife. To let it linger in Eve's
serpent-flirting eyes, to the level of the song she sang
to the birds; Eden's serpent watching, its fins
licking the corners of a poisonous mouth.
Some days I thank my mother for bringing me here.
Some days I thank my children for keeping me here.
When I am ninety, before I die,
I'll count my children's toes and fingers again.
Will they still have legs and eyes and arms then?

M-T, Turning Thirteen

My son, M-T, comes home from school,
attached to two black wires, dangling,
his arms also dangling along those long legs.
M-T dances his way through our house,
through the street, through this world, and only
the rhythmic rocking and banging as his head
rocks and his lips move will tell you

M-T is still alive. His ears connected to wires
from a band around his head, into one pocket.
Tubes hanging down my son, M-T's body.
It is a thing to see, I say, my boy no longer
connected by an umbilical cord; instead,
it is just these plastic veins carrying sounds.
My son, now gathering reinforcement

for those civil war teenage years. At school,
they all walk the same, talk the same, laugh
the same, it is no use now—we've only
cloned ourselves. Now when he passes me in
the house, I conclude, like my mother, like
my Auntie, like my mother's mother's mother's
mother, we give up our children one by one;

I say, like a woman, after all is said and done,
giving up just when the baby is finally crowned,
and coming, the baby, the hero. Labor pains
will conquer us all just the same. We scream,
"I can't do it anymore—I can-not—push!"
My son, M-T, has just been admitted into
the world, where teenagers live.

The CD boom box booms; the stereo
is his keeper. His room shakes the window
panes; the walls bang the music out in steady
vibrations through the day. At night, my
neighbor shuts her windows tight, and I say,
she has just girls, you see, just girls.
So blessed, I say, *so miserably blessed.*

Winter Street

Outside, the street stands still.
Is it the silence of the cold
or is it us?

When winter comes we turn
willing prisoners
behind closed doors.

If I holler for Gee, across the road,
no one will know this
is how a mother calls her child home.

In Monrovia, the street talks
back to us, and back and
forth, with all the passing voices;

the neighborhood is alive; and
even at night, silence
is a stranger still.

As the storm goes by,
I like the howling in the wind that drowns
the silence on this winter street.

Sometimes it takes my children
in the house to give away
what is truly me.

A Snowwoman in Her Dying Hour

for Ade-Juah

You will find her leaning sideways on my lawn—
a belt around her waist, her soft knit hat, and that

red Christmas scarf she wore for the last snowstorm
now slide slowly in the melt. Her shoulders tell

passersby how cruel this winter has been. She is so
wounded and stands without cane, without a future

or breath. She is like a woman in her old age without
children or husband or sisters or friends. Paramedics

do not come with ambulances and sirens to tend
the broken limbs of a little girl's snowwoman.

A snowwoman in her dying hour is such a crumbling
sight to behold; especially, when everyone is hollering

around the house because spring is coming in, and soon
flowers will spread sweet petals, trees will bud;

the sun will cast careless shadows about. In this jubilation,
no one cares that the snowwoman on our lawn is in her

dying hour, and her once supple body is now fluid.
When her heart stops, no one will notice how it took

all winter to build her bottom, chest, head and ground
her on that lawn. It took the pleading of a five-year-old

for her mother to help build a snowwoman who still
carries her beauty in her waistline, in her now twisted

face; and if she had been a creature endowed with hands
and fingers or claws, everyone would see how she still

stands after so many days of icy winds from the lake,
so many days of the plowman's drive-by plowing.

I Now Wander

I raised ducks, pigs, dogs, barking watchdogs.
Wild chickens loose, dancing, flapping old wings.

Red and white American roosters, meant to be sheltered
and fed with vitamins until they grow dumb;

in our yard I set them loose among African breeds
that pecked at them until they, too, grew wild and free.

I planted papayas, fat belly papayas, elongated papayas,
tiny papayas, hanging. I planted pineapples, mangoes,

long juicy sugar canes, wild coco-yams. From our bedroom
window I saw plantain and bananas bloom, again and again,

take on flesh and ripeness. And then the war came, and the rebels
slaughtered my pigs, my strong roosters, my hens,

my heavy, squawking ducks. Now I wander among strangers,
looking for new ducks, new hens, new coco-yams, new wars.

I Am Acquainted with Waiting

We waited to see if after all that smoke and shooting,
there was still us. Twelve years now,
all the anger subsiding, and again building up
among my countrymen who know how to go to war.

When Jesus hung there on the cross so many years
ago, waiting for the hour when all blood and life
would let go of him, Jesus, hanging on that cross,
his mother waiting below for the solitude hour?
Death came, comforting, like dew drops,
and then the resurrection.

After a woman has been laboring too many hours,
when the baby is finally crowned—
trust me, only the father stands jubilant at this time.
But when the waiting is done, after that last push,
after the tearing, and the baby's first cry,
when the sore mother holds her child

at her breast, trust me, how insignificant,
all that waiting. So I wait, you wait, we wait.
I am acquainted with waiting. I know the feeling
after all the flame and the smoke, after a long rainy night,
at dawn, the burnt shells of snails, the charred corpses
of scorpions, the forest fire, now quenched.
Trust me—we will return home someday, trust me.

Glossary

Abidjan. The capital city of the Ivory Coast.

Accra. The capital city of Ghana.

Ade. (Grebo) A praise name that means "our mother." It is a tradition to praise a girl named after her grandmother or mother by attaching *Ade* as a prefix to her given name.

Bai. (Grebo) Father, uncle, grandfather; also, used to address an elderly male.

Bassa Community. A neighborhood within the Capitol Bye Pass Community, near the official quarters of Liberia's capital, Monrovia.

Bati-oh-bati. (Grebo) The call or shout to order during the council meeting of elders.

Batik. An African fabric (similar to tie-dyed cloth) that is the result of a very individualized stamping and waxing process.

Bishop Brooks. Another Capitol Bye Pass neighborhood that is adjacent to Bassa Community.

Bodior. (Grebo) The high priest or spiritual head of a Grebo town within the African Traditional Religion. Anointed by ancestry, he oversees the spiritual life of the community and must descend from the family of the Bodior line. His priesthood is for life.

Bong County. One of the major counties in mid-Liberia, where one of the most populous ethnic people, the Kpelle reside. Their capital city, Gbanga, was where Charles Taylor seated his original rebel government at the beginning of the Liberian civil war.

Bony fish. Monrovia vernacular for the herring fish.

Borbor. (Grebo) Brother, uncle, male cousin, or other male relative.

Bubba. The upper part of an African dress. Similar to a blouse, it is worn with the *lappa*.

Cape Palmas. A cape at the southeastern tip of Liberia located in Harper, the capital city of Maryland County. The name Cape Palmas is important because it is used interchangeably with Harper or Maryland County. It is also significant because this cape was part of the State of Maryland in Africa until 1858, when the

Liberian government defeated the Grebos at the end of the Grebo Wars and Maryland became part of the Republic of Liberia.

Capitol Bye Pass. The main street that bypasses the nation's official headquarters.

Cassava. A root crop, sometimes called yucca root.

Charles Taylor. The rebel warlord whose guerrilla warfare (beginning in 1989) to overthrow the Samuel K. Doe government ravaged Liberia and the West African region. Taylor and his rebels were notorious for their bloody massacres and human rights abuses. Today Taylor leads Liberia amidst widespread human rights abuses and illegal diamond trading.

Craw-craw crabs. Tiny and wild crabs that live in little holes in the swamps.

Crown Hill. A neighborhood near downtown Monrovia. An important commercial section of town, especially in the 1960s.

Dorklor. (Grebo) Dance associated with the Wlee or Kahn (depending on which of the Grebo traditions one comes from). Otherwise known as the War Dance. It is a dance of celebration.

Fanti Lappa. A fine material, in any combination of colors, made of fine wax.

Gbapleh. A common fish, usually eaten by the poor.

Gbuga. A pan fish common in the rivers around Monrovia. It resembles the bluegill.

Ghana High-Life Beat. A kind of rhythmic, high-beat music originating in Ghana, which influenced much of Monrovia and other parts of city life around Africa in the 1960s.

Ghankay. The warrior name assumed by Charles Taylor. It is often used by his supporters to praise his deeds.

Grand Gedeh. A county in southeastern Liberia where Liberia's soldier-turned-president, Samuel K. Doe, originated from. It is home to the Krahn ethnic people, whose defense of Doe cost them heavily in the war.

Grebo/Glebo. An ethnic people from the southeastern Liberian county of Maryland. The Grebos are one of the most prominent ethnic groups in Liberia. The Grebo language is part of the Kwa family of languages in Liberia and West Africa.

Gronna-girls. Vernacular for girls who have no parental control to guide them and are sometimes referred to as "loose girls." The word for such male youths is *gronna-boys.* "Gronna" comes from the word "grown-up," but connotatively means someone who has grown up without proper upbringing.

Gbor-belloh. Professionally trained magician, spiritist, artist, and seer. His role as entertainer often allows him also to dress up like a clown.

Harmattan. The cold, dry January winds that blow across West Africa from the Sahara Desert.

Harper. The capital city of Maryland County.

Iyeeh. Grandmother or mother; also used to describe an elderly woman.

Kaluway. A group of Grebo people composed of families living in eight towns, located about thirty miles west of Harper.

Khade-wheh. (Grebo) A praise name used to describe a great woman or girl. It means "head wife" or "great mother."

The Killing Rubber Bush. A killing field area near the Soul Clinic Mission displaced center where my family and I lived. This was one of dozens of killing grounds for Taylor's rebels, where there was a mountain of executed civilians. We smelled the dead from this bush daily as we lived in the displaced center.

Kinja. A rattan-crafted carrier for wood or goods.

Kru. An ethnic people whose main homeland is Sinoe County. It is among the most prominent of the ethnic groups of Liberia. The Kru language is part of the Kwa family of languages.

Kwashiorkor. A wasting disease that is caused by an insufficient intake of protein and chiefly affects young children in tropical countries, producing apathy, edema of the extremities, desquamation, and partial loss of pigmentation (and generally associated with diarrhea and stunted growth), leading in severe cases to death.

Lappa. The wrap-around or skirt that is worn by most African women.

The Liberian civil war. The Liberian civil war began in December 1989 when armed rebels led by their warlord, Charles Taylor, invaded the nation in the most ruthless warfare seen in West Africa since the end of colonialism. The war ravaged much of the country, killing over a quarter million and displacing more than a million of the prewar 2.5 million Liberians. Despite its atrocities, the war received only brief coverage in the international news, and most of the suffering civilians were left to fend for themselves during much of the war. The war officially ended in August 1996 with the implementation of the Abuja Peace Accord in Nigeria. IIn 1997, the chief rebel leader took power despite much opposition from half a dozen other rebel factions. Taylor was supposedly elected by a majority and has since reigned over his country with terror. In 2001, the United Nations imposed an economic and travel embargo on Taylor and his government. The embargo was intended to stop the Liberian rebel leader from supporting rebels in Sierra Leone with an arms-for-diamond trade. Today, Taylor continues to rule Liberia despite continuing human rights abuses, and the international human rights organizations have called on him to end the violence.

Mesurado. The river that runs through greater Monrovia and into the suburbs.

"Na Nyebioh, Nyankeh Hne, Na Nyebioh." (Grebo) ("My Husband, Nyankeh Hne, My Husband") a popular and classical Grebo love song in which a young woman is pleading to her husband to take responsibility for the child both of them have brought into the world.

Nimba. A county in northeastern Liberia, now well-known for its support of Charles Taylor's war against Samuel K. Doe. The willingness of the people there to be used by Taylor in his rebel warfare caused them much loss of life and disillusionment over the last decade.

Po-po-wlee-oh. (Grebo) A cry for the dead, often used to call the living to attention when disaster strikes.

Sagba. (Grebo) A praise name given to women. This was my stepmother's praise name.

Second Mourning. A time of mourning in black and white instead of in pure black. It is the tradition in much of Liberia to go through the two stages of mourning, something required by the culture.

Sinoe. A county in the southern region of Liberia where the Kru ethnic people reside.

Slip Way. A small community at the edge of the Mesurado River, beneath the bulging Crown Hill Community.

Soul Clinic Refugee Camp. A boarding school facility where my family and I fled to and lived with thousands of other displaced people during the war in Monrovia. It is noted as one of the places where Charles Taylor's men carried out some of the worst massacres and executions of civilians in both 1990 and 1991.

The Mat. A large mat, which according to Grebo tradition, is spread out for mourners to sit upon and wail for a week or so for the dead. It is an abomination not to lay The Mat down when a family member has died. The Mat is also a symbolic bearer of all the grief.

Total Involvement Suit. The nickname for a style of French suits that was popularized in Liberia by Liberia's nineteenth president, William R. Tolbert, while he was in office. In 1971, when President Tolbert was sworn into office, his style of dress—a white, short-sleeved, French-style suit—inspired Liberian elites to wear this modern African style instead of traditional westernized styles. Unlike his predecessor, President Tubman, who wore the western, black, three-piece suit, Tolbert was never seen wearing anything but a white French suit. The suit became known as the "Swear-in-Suit" and later became known as the "Total Involvement Suit" when Tolbert developed his national motto of "Total Involvement for Higher Heights." People began calling his suit and all French-style male coat suits the "Total Involvement Suit." President William R. Tolbert was assassinated on April 12, 1980, in a military coup that brought Samuel K. Doe into power. Tolbert was said to be wearing his French suit when he was shot that morning.

Tugbakeh. My hometown, located about thirty miles from the coastal city of Harper. It is occupied by the Grebo people who speak the Tuobo dialect of the Grebo language. It is also home to the Pentecostal Mission, which began work in the 1940s. In the 1980s, Tugbakeh became the headquarters of the New Tribes Mission project based in Liberia. My great-grandfathers founded the first village that was the original Tugbakeh more than 150 years ago.

Wahnjeh. (Grebo) A praise name for a woman.

Wlansu. (Grebo) A praise name for a woman. This was my mother's praise name.

Yana Boys. Petty retailers who travel around town, selling clothing or pots or other housewares. *Yana boys* were popular in the 1960s during the rise of commerce and the days of traveling salesmen. They are now becoming extinct as more peddlers and retailers settle into huge marketplaces like Waterside in Monrovia.

Other Books in the Crab Orchard Award Series in Poetry

Muse
Susan Aizenberg

This Country of Mothers
Julianna Baggott

White Summer
Joelle Biele

In Search of the Great Dead
Richard Cecil

Names above Houses
Oliver de la Paz

The Star-Spangled Banner
Denise Duhamel

Pelican Tracks
Elton Glaser

Winter Amnesties
Elton Glaser

Fabulae
Joy Katz

Train to Agra
Vandana Khanna

Crossroads and Unholy Water
Marilene Phipps

Misery Prefigured
J. Allyn Rosser